Limerick County Library

30012 00654895 1

WITHDRAWN FROM STOCK

KU-190-430

PC8P3306

MYTHICAL CREATURES

Unicorns

Limerick
County Library
00654895

Abby Colich

www.raintreepublishers.co.uk
Visit our website to find out more information about Raintree books.

To order:
☎ Phone 0845 6044371
📄 Fax +44 (0) 1865 312263
💻 Email myorders@raintreepublishers.co.uk

Customers from outside the UK please telephone +44 1865 312262

Raintree is an imprint of Capstone Global Library Limited, a company incorporated in England and Wales having its registered office at 7 Pilgrim Street, London, EC4V 6LB – Registered company number: 6695582

Text © Capstone Global Library Limited 2011
First published in hardback in 2011
The moral rights of the proprietor have been asserted.

All rights reserved. No part of this publication may be reproduced in any form or by any means (including photocopying or storing it in any medium by electronic means and whether or not transiently or incidentally to some other use of this publication) without the written permission of the copyright owner, except in accordance with the provisions of the Copyright, Designs and Patents Act 1988 or under the terms of a licence issued by the Copyright Licensing Agency, Saffron House, 6–10 Kirby Street, London EC1N 8TS (www.cla.co.uk). Applications for the copyright owner's written permission should be addressed to the publisher.

Edited by Adrian Vigliano, Rebecca Rissman, and Nancy Dickmann
Designed by Joanna Hinton Malivoire
Levelling by Jeanne Clidas
Original illustrations by Christian Slade
Original illustrations © Capstone Global Library
Picture research by Elizabeth Alexander
Production by Victoria Fitzgerald
Originated by Capstone Global Library
Printed and bound in China by CTPS

ISBN 978 1 4062 1648 6 (hardback)
14 13 12 11 10
10 9 8 7 6 5 4 3 2 1

British Library Cataloguing in Publication Data
Colich, Abby.
Unicorns. -- (Mythical creatures)
398.4'69-dc22
A full catalogue record for this book is available from the British Library.

Acknowledgements
We would like to thank the following for permission to reproduce photographs: Alamy pp. **17** (© Hemis), **18** (© ArkReligion.com); Bridgeman pp. **11** (National Museum of Karachi, Karachi, Pakistan), **24** (Private Collection/ © Look and Learn); Corbis pp. **9** (© Stapleton Collection), **21** (© The Gallery Collection), **22** (© Alinari Archives), **29** (© Buddy Mays); Getty Images pp. **7** (Hulton Archive), **28** (Paul Nicklen/National Geographic); Photolibrary pp. **13** (Stapleton Historical Collection/Imagestate), **23** (E&E Image Library/Imagestate), **25** (DEA Picture Library); Shutterstock pp. **8** (© vincent369), **10** (© Linn Currie).

Every effort has been made to contact copyright holders of material reproduced in this book. Any omissions will be rectified in subsequent printings if notice is given to the publisher.

Disclaimer
All the Internet addresses (URLs) given in this book were valid at the time of going to press. However, due to the dynamic nature of the Internet, some addresses may have changed, or sites may have changed or ceased to exist since publication. While the author and publisher regret any inconvenience this may cause readers, no responsibility for any such changes can be accepted by either the author or the publisher.

Some words are shown in bold, **like this**. You can find out what they mean by looking in the glossary.

Contents

What is a mythical creature?

People all over the world tell stories about **mythical** creatures. The word *mythical* comes from the word *myth*. A myth is a story that is not true.

This is a dragon. It is a mythical creature.

Limerick County Library

What other mythical creatures can you think of?

werewolf

What is a unicorn?

What comes to mind when you think of a unicorn? You may have seen unicorns that look like a white horse with one horn.

Unicorns can have the body of many different animals. But they always have one horn.

The unicorn's special powers

Many **legends** say that the unicorn's horn has special powers. Others say that the unicorn brings people peace, strength, and bravery.

Chinese unicorn statues

DID YOU KNOW?

In some **myths**, unicorns are very hard to catch!

The unicorn myth

Myths about the unicorn began thousands of years ago. Stories about the unicorn probably come from horned animals such as:

- antelopes
- deer
- goats
- oxen
- rhinoceroses

rhinoceros

This is a very old clay artwork of a unicorn. It was made between 4,500 and 3,700 years ago.

Ancient Greek writers

The first people to tell stories of unicorns were the Greeks. One story says that unicorns have the body of a donkey. It also says that unicorns have dark red heads with blue eyes. Their horns are white, red, and black.

Ancient Greece

DID YOU KNOW?

The Greeks named a group of stars monoceros (say *mon-oh-sare-us*). *Monoceros* is the Greek word for unicorn.

Unicorns of the Middle East

Middle East

Iran

Legends from the Middle East tell us about a unicorn called the karkadaan (say *car-kuh-dan*). It was a fierce creature that could kill an elephant. The word *karkadaan* means "lord of the desert".

DID YOU KNOW?

People from Persia, now called Iran, believed in a unicorn called the Shadhavar (say *shad-huh-var*). Its **hollow** horn makes music and has a face on it.

Unicorns of Asia

One **legend** in India tells of a creature called Risharinga (say *rish-ah-ring-ah*). He was the son of a man and an antelope. Stories say Risharinga married a princess named Shanta (say *shan-tah*). He saved her father's kingdom from **drought**.

Risharinga

Shanta

Asia

China →

Japan

India →

DID YOU KNOW?
Indian unicorn stories might have started because of the Indian rhinoceros.

Legends in Asia tell about a creature called the Qilin (say *kee-lin*). There are many stories about what the Qilin looks like. But most say it has scales and a horn.

This is a Qilin from China.

kirin

DID YOU KNOW?
The Qilin has many different names. In Japan it is called the kirin (say *kee-rin*).

Unicorns of Europe

There are many **legends** about unicorns in **medieval** Europe. These unicorns usually looked like a goat or a horse with a horn. Some people believed that powder made from a unicorn horn could protect them from poison and cure diseases.

Germany

Europe

This well-known cloth from medieval Europe shows a woman and a unicorn.

Limerick County Library
00654895

Myths tell us that unicorns are hard to catch! In some stories, a unicorn can be caught if it lays its head on a **maiden's** lap. Some stories say that unicorns come back to life after being killed.

Unicorns and lions are used in family symbols. Unicorns make people feel strong and brave.

DID YOU KNOW?
Einhorn is the German word for unicorn.

Close relatives

A **mythical** creature that is like the unicorn is Pegasus. Like some unicorns, Pegasus has the body of a horse. But Pegasus has wings and no horn.

DID YOU KNOW?

These ancient **extinct** animals are named after a mythical beast called the indrik (say *in-drick*). Russian **myths** say the indrik lived on a mountain and ruled all animals.

Could unicorns exist?

 They could be real...

- People all over the world tell stories about unicorns.

 I'm not so sure...

- These stories were probably made up about real animals that had one horn.

 They could be real...

- Some people claim they have found unicorn horns.

 I'm not so sure...

- These horns were actually **tusks** from a sea animal called the narwhal.

26

They could be real...

- **Legends** say that unicorns are difficult to capture. They might just be really good at hiding from humans.

 I'm not so sure...

- No one has ever actually seen a unicorn.

There are many interesting stories about unicorns. What do you think?

Reality versus myth

Narwhal (real)

Found: Arctic Ocean

Lives: in water

Seen: rarely by humans

Special power: finds its way using **echolocation.**

Narwhals are sometimes called "unicorns of the sea." They are whales with a long, spiralled **tusk**.

Unicorn (myth)

Found: in stories from Asia, Europe, and the Middle East

Lives: on land

Seen: in films and art

Special power: protects people from poison and disease.

Glossary

drought when a place has almost no rain or water

echolocation using the sound of echoes to find the way

extinct has completely died out

hollow not filled with anything

legend traditional story that may or may not be true

maiden an unmarried woman

medieval time in Europe from around the year 500 to around the year 1500

myth traditional story, often about magical creatures and events

mythical found in myths

tusk a long tooth that grows from the jaw of some animals. Some tusks look like horns.

Find out more

Books

I Believe in Unicorns (book and CD), Michael Morpurgo (Walker Books, 2007)

Monsterology, Dugald Steer (Templar Publishing, 2008)

The Orchard Book of the Unicorn and Other Magical Animals, Margaret Mayo (Orchard Books, 2008)

Websites

www.amnh.org/exhibitions/mythiccreatures/
The American Museum of Natural History's Mythic Creature exhibit website has lots of information about creatures of the land, sky, and water.

www.fieldmuseum.org/mythiccreatures/index.html
Learn about dragons, unicorns, and mermaids at the Field Museum's Mythic Creatures Exhibit website.

Index